IMAGES
of America

BAYPORT
HERITAGE

Homan's Creek at sunset.

IMAGES
of America

BAYPORT
HERITAGE

Bayport Heritage Association

ARCADIA

First published 1997
Reprinted 2004

Published by Arcadia Publishing,
an imprint of Tempus Publishing Inc.
Portsmouth NH, Charleston SC, Chicago,
San Francisco

Printed in Great Britain

For all general information, contact Arcadia Publishing:
Telephone 843-853-2070
Fax 843-853-0044
E-mail sales@arcadiapublishing.com
For customer service and orders:
Toll-free 1-888-313-2665

Visit us on the Internet at www.arcadiapublishing.com

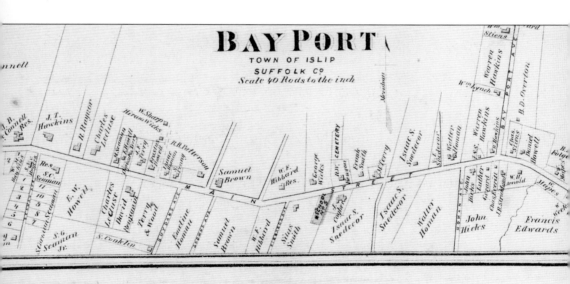

Map of Bayport, circa 1873.

Contents

Acknowledgments

Researched, compiled, and presented by the following members of the
Bayport Heritage Association:

Donald H. Weinhardt, chairman
Denise McFadden, vice-chairman
Alden Olsson
Flo Olsson
Irma Reilly
June Gillette
Marion Cohn
Hervey Connell

In particular we acknowledge and thank all the contributors who searched their family albums, and post card collections and graciously donated to the Bayport Heritage Association's archives: Gisbert Auwaeter, The Bayport Fire Dept., Marion Beebe, William Bielitz, Henry Betjemann, Charles H.J. Bogel, Peter Brewer, Alan Brown, Raphael Del Castillo, Nancy Cozine, Catharine M. Denning, Charles Dickerson, Ruth Dougherty, Mary Ege, Fred Eveland, James Gillette, June Gillette, Mary Jones Gillette, Anna Huston Golden, Constance Haab, Hans Henke, Eleanor Hester, Viola Imhof, Betty Kuss, Herb Lipson, Barney Loughlin, Denise McFadden, Alexandra Merwin, Gail Merwin, Edith Miller, Alden & Flo Olsson, Stanley Orenkewicz, Althea Palmer, Alice Parks, Eileen Petersen, Dan Pichney, Ruth Platt, Ken & Virginia Poli, Waldron K. Post, Betty Prall, Calvin T. Pratt, Peggy Primavera, Ken Purdy, Irma Reilly, Robert Reilly, Ann & Hazel Savage, Sayville Historical Society, James Shand, Society for the Preservation of Long Island Antiquities, Carl Starace, The Suffolk County Parks, Division of Historic Services, Everett Trochelman, Ruth Vanik, Don & Carol Weinhardt, Jane Glacken Westfield, Lavern Wittlock, Sr., Ron Ziel, and anyone we may have unwittingly overlooked.

Introduction

The area now known as Bayport was originally inhabited by the Secatogue Indians, who lived on the south shore of Long Island from Massapequa to Patchogue. They were the original fishermen, clam diggers, and sailors of this area. The arrival of the first Europeans brought with it disease and death to a population with no tolerance or immunity to such a new threat. One population almost exclusively wiped out the other and few Native Americans remained in this coastline area.

The new settlers did not need to travel any farther. They quickly realized the treasure they had come upon; fertile land and abundant sea. Through the patent of 1697, William Nicoll obtained the area today encompassing Bayport, Sayville, West Sayville, Holbrook, and Ronkonkoma, all within the town of Islip. Much of the area's economy was derived from the bay, and an interesting dilemma began when Nicoll, in applying for the patent, inadvertently excluded the Great South Bay bottom. These valuable lands remain part of Brookhaven Town to the present time.

In the year 1780, William Nicoll III died, and stipulated in his will that no subdivision of his inherited land take place until his great-grandson reached the age of twenty-one. However, his son, William Nicoll IV, found it necessary to settle his debts and sought to override his father's will in order to sell part of the family's land holdings. In an attempt to raise the sum of 4,000£, a parcel of land which represented the western third of present-day Bayport, south of Montauk Highway, was sold to Jeremiah Terry. Very shortly thereafter Gersham Hawkins purchased the center portion of Bayport, south of Montauk Highway. These 1786 transactions resulted in the creation of Bayport.

In 1733 South Country Road, now known as Montauk Highway, was laid out, and by 1790 the Federal Census indicated that about ten families were residing in Bayport. It was in this year, on April 22, that George Washington passed through Bayport along the South Country Road during his tour of Long Island.

In 1820 William Nicoll VI reached the age of twenty-one and in the period between 1820 and 1823 he provided "quit-claim" deeds to lands previously conveyed in Bayport to, among others, William C. Smith, John Hawkins, William Brown, Benjamin Birdsall, Isaac Brown, and William Arthur. The sale of these lands and the subsequent creation of farms gave the community stability and permanence, and in January 1832, the residents petitioned the Commissioner of Roads to open, to standard legal width, a road through the center of Bayport that had previously existed as a path or lane since 1814. This remains as the present-day Middle Road.

The early years of the nineteenth century were known as the "pine wood" era. A great demand for wood in New York City kept the locals busy cutting and carting. In the late 1830s, however, both the supply and demand for wood diminished. New ways to make a living were sought. The resources of the Great South Bay offered one important alternative. In addition, the land that had been cleared of trees was used for farming, with fish and seaweed from the bay being used as fertilizer. By 1850 approximately fifty-six families resided in Bayport and 70% of them were dependent on farming or the bay for employment. During this time the community called itself Middle Roadville or Southport. The name Bayport was not officially used until 1871.

The decade prior to the Civil War saw fairly steady growth. The children of the early settlers were now old enough to marry and start their own families. By and large they stayed close to home and the Census records for 1860 indicate seventy households in the area. Several members of the community fought in the Civil War. The years following the war brought significant changes to the community, including the arrival of the railroad in 1869, which opened up the south shore of Long Island as a renowned summer resort. The development of photography took place in time to capture a flavor of the pomp and allure of this period. It is indeed with great appreciation and interest that we re-examine Bayport's early photographic legacy. This medium came just in time to capture earlier structures that now have disappeared, and has put faces to and given life to this historical text. The emphasis in the remaining pages is a presentation of what those before us made extra effort to preserve.

The remainder of the story of Bayport can be pictorially told in terms of its service and social institutions: its schools, church, post office, and fire department; its economic life, including general stores, the railroad, and the floriculture business; and with an intimate peek into its homes and people, their life and leisure, and the way they, together, form what we remember as and call Bayport.

Bayport Village , cir. 1908

The stage is set, the ready land waits, amply forested, fertile, yielding game as large as deer, as plentiful as rabbit, and as satisfying as quail. The bay swells and recedes, abundant with flounder and fluke, oysters, blue claw crabs, and clams ready for harvest, spilling over with bounty left waiting upon the shore.

One

A Beginning:
The Early Years

The stage is indeed set, people have come and chosen to stay. Early stirrings and indications suggest Bayport is being born . . .

Traces of our early years remain, co-existing side by side with signs of our expansion, growth, and maturity. Take a moment to travel down Middle Road and notice, in reflection, from where we've come.

This is the beginning of Bayport on Middle Road. Traveling east one enters Bayport at a quaint point where you would naturally hesitate, to more gently cross over the slight rise as the road bridges Brown's River. You look to clear the parked bikes or the pulled-over van, and smile at the diversity of the setting—the youngsters crabbing, or the lone man fishing. The scene is rural and natural, and unobtrusive to the environmental panorama.

This is the same bridge crossing, looking west, circa 1908, with an early vehicle leaving the tree-lined drive of Meadow Croft, John E. Roosevelt's estate bordering Bayport. The caretaker's son, Barney Loughlin, found this photograph in his family's album. From this point eastward, Bayport's first house of early note comes into view.

Weathered and behind a privacy of unattended hedges stands the "Green House" at 328 Middle Road. It is immediately to the south and bordering the eastern bank of Brown's River. Built in 1889, it was described as one of the best built and neatest cottages in the vicinity. Of more importance, it stands as one of the few remaining examples of a "bayman's" cottage. Captured in a frozen moment in time, Morris and Pinky Green, baymen themselves, stop to pose.

One block further, also on the south side, and at the southeast corner of Seaman Avenue, sits the charming circa 1835 farmhouse of Silas Carman Seaman. He was a sea captain, born in 1803, who had fourteen children, and lived to the ripe old age of eighty-three.

Alice Seaman Benjamin was one of the generations of Seamans to grow up here. She was the grand-daughter of Silas, the daughter of John, and married Norman Benjamin on September 20, 1907. It seemed newsworthy for the local paper to print that the couple left their wedding reception in an auto, for Babylon, where they took a train.

ANANDA HALL
MIDDLEROAD
BAYPORT, L.I.

This home, circa 1870, once owned by an early Bayport schoolteacher and later serving as a summer boarding house called Ananda Hall, still stands at number 365, on the north side of Middle Road. Subsequently, the structure fell into disrepair, even housing a squatter. The Moore family purchased it in 1981 and lovingly brought back its original charm, only to see it damaged by a fire sparked by lightning in 1985. Repairs were re-done and it stands a phoenix, having risen once again.

This circa 1830 home was resold in 1835 with one acre of property for $120. In 1887 a Victorian kitchen extension was added to the north side. It is easy to see why this early home on the northwest corner of Oakwood Avenue and Middle Road once served most charmingly as a "Tea House" in the 1920s. In 1967, fire damaged the building to such a degree that it was taken down, but a faithful reproduction (including the original windows) was built to a slightly larger scale.

12

As a young woman, Libby Homan (1848–97) left Bayport a treasure in keeping a diary during the days her mother ran a boarding house in the residence seen below.

According to the 1858 map of Bayport, this two-story residence already existed on the northeast corner of Oakwood Avenue and Middle Road. Previously boasting a third story, this proud structure has seen use as a residence, a store, a boarding house, and a hotel.

N°3669 THE EUREKA HOUSE, BAYPORT, L. I.

The site of 407 Middle Road was part of the original Brown Homestead purchased by William Brown in 1787. This 40-acre parcel was sold to William Needham of Brooklyn for $4,000 in 1873. The Needhams ran a summer boarding house there called the "Needham Hotel," as depicted in this photograph.

Lawrence Edwards came to Bayport from Barbados, West Indies. In 1846 he purchased a 160-acre farm from Jacob Smith. This is a photograph of the original homestead, one of the earliest homes in Bayport, which stood on the north side of Middle Road on what is today "Bayport Commons." In 1867 the building was moved to Sayville to the south side of Middle Road, just east of the library. Plans were being made for its new home at the Restoration Village Grange on Broadway Avenue, Sayville, when it was lost to fire on Christmas night, 1975, the unfortunate result of vandalism.

Lawrence Edwards built this lovely Greek Revival home at 463 Middle Road for his son, Lawrence Barnes Edwards, and his wife Margaret circa 1852. This property was a one-acre portion of the 160 acres conveyed to Mr. Edwards from Jacob Smith in 1846. In 1905 a new porch was added and the noteworthy innovation for the time was installed—electricity.

This is the third house built by Lawrence Edwards for one of his children, his daughter Mary and her husband, Franklin B. Smith. The house, which stands at 473 Middle Road, was found to have seaweed insulation. Proximity to the Great South Bay yielded many practical benefits.

On the 1858 map of Bayport this house was shown in the ownership of John Hawkins. The structure also became home to John's son, the Coger family, and John Hamburger, who along with his brother ran a woolen mill business in the barn in the back yard, until the barn and business were destroyed by fire. The United Methodist Church purchased the property circa 1955 and for several years used the house as a Sunday school. Pressure for additional parking ultimately caused the demolition of the structure in 1963.

This building stood on the north side of Middle Road across from what is now Bayport Memorial Park. In 1840, when Daniel and Nancy Howell conveyed a 50-acre farm to Charles Homan, the house, or part of it, probably was in existence. During an interesting period in its colorful life, while Charles' son, Walter Homan, served as postmaster, part of this building was Bayport's fourth post office (1892–1894).

This house stood on the northwest corner of Middle Road and Bayport Avenue as early as 1858. Warren Hawkins was the owner. In 1885 Hawkins sold 4 acres on the corner, including the dwelling, to Captain Isaac Snedecor. The porch was added in 1894 and sometime after 1946 the building was demolished to make way for a gas station.

This house at 647 Middle Road was built some time before 1834. In the 1880s the place was fondly called "Linden Cottage." The old Linden tree was brought down in the infamous 1938 hurricane. While renovating in the 1980s, the current occupants found items within the old walls that had been purposely left there waiting to be rediscovered; the contents within included a bisque doll, hand-blown bottle, and an old-fashioned wooden ice skate.

The impressive home now hidden behind the hedges on the northeast corner of Ocean Avenue and Middle Road once looked like the one above. In 1875, it was the farm complex of Frank Smith. Major renovations in 1893 created a grander look. The house was moved back, turned, and an entirely new section was added.

From this view we can see how the home at 677 Middle Road looked originally. It was built sometime between 1876 and 1880. George E. Smith lived there; he was the village blacksmith and had his shop near where number 626 Middle Road is today, the prior site of Ma Moon's restaurant.

Eva Gillette lived in the house below at 719 Middle Road. Her attention to making note of local history has been of special value to the Bayport Heritage Association.

This property at 719 Middle Road was part of a farm as early as 1813, and passed from members of the Jayne family, the Wicks family, and the Mazaurie family, who conveyed it to Edgar Gillette. After Edgar the property was owned by his son Edward, then by Edward's wife, Mary Gillette, and eventually by their daughter Eva in 1916.

Timber from an old ship wreck off Fire Island was used in the construction of this circa 1851 Gillette family house at 727 Middle Road. It originally was a part of an earlier, more extensive farm owned by Zebulon Gillette; Edgar Gillette had built this structure originally for the hired men.

Here the Gillette children Frances, Ambrose Rene, and Lois enjoy each other's company and find the joy in a summer's day.

Part of this farm operation is the horse-powered treadmill we see here, most probably driving a threshing machine. How interesting it is that they thought to photograph these types of images.

This is a hand-driven fanning mill, also called a winnowing machine. Winnowing is the process of separating or freeing the chaff from the grain by means of wind or driven air. This machine was also part of the Gillette farm.

Records from 1870 indicate an Edgar Gillette living in this circa 1812 farm house at 747 Middle Road; by the time the above photograph was taken, alterations had been made and Edgar's daughter and her husband, Moses McMath, lived here. Moses and Emma Jane are the couple to the right.

This old barn, sketched by Henry Betjemann, once stood on the northeast corner of Gillette Avenue and Middle Road in Bayport. Even though in a state of "ruin" such structures continued to benefit and enrich their surroundings until removed by "progress."

In 1849, Isaac S. Snedecor, a retired sea captain, came to Bayport from Oakdale and bought a farm with a house from John and Jennie Hawkins. He lived and raised his family here until 1879. This old red farmhouse was then cut in two, with the front section being moved from the site of number 515 Middle Road to its present location at 282 Snedecor Avenue, just north of the railroad tracks. Pictured here is the Edward Gillette family, occupying the home circa 1902.

Titje and John Beintema came from Holland and rented this home, which at the time was seventy-five years old. After this picture was taken in 1907, the family had another child, resulting in a total of nine. John started with three cows in Bayport and moved on to owning the Southside Dairy in West Sayville. This building, along with its outbuildings, was still standing in 1946, on the north side of Montauk Highway between Lakewood and McConnell Avenues. The site is now occupied by the Sans Souci Condominiums.

This little Bayport girl sits posed in Sunday finery. Her family, the Stiens, were early settlers in Bayport who started the ice dispensing business here, planted the long row of graceful trees still lining Bayport Avenue, and in the early 1900s owned and operated Stiens Bayport Carousel.

Two
Transportation:
Wheels of Time

Unquestionably, the coming of the railroad, now bringing within reasonable distance the metropolis of New York City and the rural charm of Bayport, was the single most influential event for Bayport's future.

The Southside Railroad first came through Bayport in 1869, bringing and creating dramatic changes in the community. Much land that was originally dedicated to agriculture was now developed for summer leisure, enjoyed by local residents, and wealthy "city" dwellers looking for a quick escape. The town came alive from June to Labor Day with summer guests, some of whom rented rooms from local townspeople. In 1884 the Long Island Rail Road listed Bayport as having accommodations for 296 guests in various homes and boarding houses. The distance from each residence to the Great South Bay was indicated in the LIRR brochure since the bay was the great attraction in Bayport!

The original site of the railroad station was east of Bayport Avenue and south of the tracks. Our view of this station was taken at the end of its use, circa 1903. The building behind was the Frieman's Hotel, now the Bayport House Ristorante, which was built in 1888. William B. Arthur, of Blue Point, had his house moved to Bayport and situated on the east side of Bayport Avenue, north of the tracks (now the Salt Box Realty). He operated a general store and was the first stationmaster and postmaster.

By 1903 a new and larger station was needed, and the site was moved to west of Snedecor Avenue on the south side of the tracks. Land was donated by Mrs. Edward Gillette and a concrete-covered brick station was built, costing $8,000. Station agent Leslie Davis is pictured here at the new station with Mrs. Davis and their children, Stanley and Ida.

This photograph of the Bayport Depot is dated August 1, 1906. The waiting horse-drawn carriages and gentlemen suggest a fully active station.

With manicured landscaping, the Bayport Railroad Station grew to be impressively welcoming. Unfortunately, the number of daily commuters eventually no longer warranted the upkeep of such a station and this fine building was ultimately demolished and replaced with a metal shed. Now the metal shed is gone and the trains merely whistle at crossings while going through Bayport.

This steam locomotive passenger train, circa 1938, is arriving at the Bayport station.

This photograph, dated July 6, 1972, shows a diesel passenger train heading westbound at Bayport Avenue.

The George Giroux family and their convertible are shown here in a close-up taken in front of 89 McConnell Avenue.

This sleek trotting horse and his master, probably Wilson R. Smith, are in front of the Smith barn on Ocean Avenue. This location is now number 661 Middle Road.

This photograph from the summer of 1909 shows the luxurious car probably owned by the family posing in dusters.

Dusters were not only fashionable, but a necessity on the dirt roads of Bayport as the age of the automobile began. This group posed in front of the houses at 89 and 87 McConnell Avenue in 1910. The homes, though enlarged and modified, are there still.

One horse, a two-man buggy, and Sunday finery mark this spring outing. This picture, circa 1915, was taken in the rear of the John Strickland home on Middle Road, Bayport. The house in the center of this picture is the back of the Charles W. Evarts house which is now the Bayport Deli. The tower of the old Bayport Firehouse can be seen over the house on the left.

Surreys did exist with a fringe on top. This 1906 picture was taken on McConnell Avenue.

This circa 1909 water wagon was important in keeping the dust down on Bayport's dirt roads. Characteristic of this bayfront area were oyster-shell roads along with the dirt. On a hot, dry day, the dust from crushed oyster shells would permeate the air like dry chalk, and the water wagons became essential for wetting things down. The view is on McConnell Avenue.

A marvelous new "motor car," circa 1905, sits in front of 34 South Ocean Avenue, Bayport.

The trolley was run by the Suffolk Traction Company, and the fare was 10¢. The view in this photograph shows car #1 approaching the Bayport Railroad Station at Snedecor Avenue. Bayport Avenue is in the background. The year is 1913. The route from Blue Point was west on Railroad Avenue to the Bayport station, then west to Oakwood Avenue to Middle Road, then west on Middle Road to Sayville.

Headed toward Bayport, this trolley ran into an intense traffic jam under the railroad trestle spanning Blue Point Avenue in Blue Point.

THOMAS E. WEEKS
DEALER IN
NEWSPAPERS AND MAGAZINES

TELEPHONE CONNECTION

BAYPORT, N. Y. Sept 7 1913

The first trolley car from Bluepoint to Bay Port on Sunday Sept 7 - 1913, at 3.20 P.M. Car No 3 the people to come in on this car was John R Woods, John O. Savercool and Frank P. Wright, the first ones to leave on this car were Frank Arnda and wife,

The first day this car run on a regular schedule was Sept 8 - 1913 at 12.20 P.M. Thomas E Weeks and wife rode over to Patchogue on this car the first day it ran on a regular schedule time Sept 8 - 1913

As noted, the first trolley from Blue Point to Bayport ran on Sunday, September 7, 1913, at 3:20 pm. Three gentlemen came in on the car, and one married couple got back on—quite a success! As the trolley proved its worth, even high school students used this means of transportation to go to either Sayville High School or Patchogue High School, since Bayport did not yet have its own four-year high school.

Three

Estates and Summer Homes:
The Resort Era

The advancement in transportation, and in particular the railroad, brought wealthier vacationers and investors to the area, and paved the way for, first summer, and then more permanent, prestigious residences to dot the area and begin to replace open farmland.

This is an early view looking toward the bay down South Ocean Avenue. On the 1834 map of Bayport the road appears, but without a name. On the 1858 map it is called Edward's Lane. In 1880, residents of the village decided to change the name to "Ocean Avenue" and placed an inscribed sign upon the road declaring it so.

These lopped trees, still found here along South Ocean Avenue, were purposely encouraged to grow in this formation as permanent boundary indicators for early farms. They serve now as an unusually intriguing entry-way leading down an avenue lined with impressive former summer homes and wealthy estates, occupying the very sites of the original early farms.

J.W. Meeks, son of a prominent furniture manufacturer, purchased this property from Edward Edwards and built this impressive Italianate-style Victorian as a summer retreat, at 22 South Ocean Avenue, in 1881. An interesting tower addition was constructed seven years later. Notice the bicycle ready for use—a popular novelty for the time.

The Cleveland Pratt house, at 102 South Ocean Avenue, along with its outbuildings was built in 1885 for $8,000 and used primarily as a summer residence. It was completely destroyed by fire 110 years later, and was then replaced by a contemporary Victorian.

Along the same avenue, of note is number 78, built in 1879 for John Morgan of the "White Rock" company. The property was also purchased from Edward Edwards.

How fortunate we are to have an interior view of 78 South Ocean Avenue, detailing casual refinement, the atmosphere and feeling of the wealthy striving for a comfortable retreat.

Set among the summer residences of wealthy families from Manhattan, great estates graced many Bayport avenues. The Stoppani-Manton summer estate, built in 1897, handsomely draws attention here on the east side of South Ocean Avenue at number 133. In its original days, the estate was named "Liberty Hall"; later, when owned by Judge Manton, it was called "Fairacres."

Originally stretching from street to street, the estate property included several outbuildings, including the charming carriage house, now a separate residence, at 90 South Fairview Avenue.

The "Fairacres" formal gardens pictured in the above photograph attest to a sense of stateliness achieved in the planning of some of Bayport's summer estates.

On the same estate, the sprawling greenhouse pictured above exemplified those gracing other private estates, before the greenhouse industry became a part of the Bayport commercial scene.

At the west foot of South Ocean Avenue, and viewed from crafts on the Great South Bay, stood "Strandhome," the estate of Charles A. Post.

Originally built in 1887 for $35,000, this impressive structure served as a summer home. The estate continued in the Post family until 1953, when 22 acres were sold and subdivision plans resulted in the demolition of the main house.

A carriage house with windmill on top, a caretaker's cottage, a barn, and a shed are among outbuildings to this complex estate.

This wonderful photograph shows the porch area of "Strandhome." The telescope seen here is a reminder of C.A. Post's interest in astronomy.

One of the features of this estate was a complete observatory which was eventually given to Harvard University.

This interior view of "Strandhome" demonstrates warmth, wealth, and masculinity. Dark finished natural woodwork, oriental rugs, and a very ornate fireback in the hearth are some items of note. A sword and two pistols below the mantel and above it another sword plus two fencing swords, beer steins, and a Toby pitcher give us some sense of the recreational inclinations of the head of the household.

Mary Lawrence Perkins Post shared her husband's commitment to serving the community, and was a volunteer at the local Red Cross.

Waldron Kintzing Post, a Harvard graduate and lawyer, was the 1951 recipient of the American Legion community service award, a charter member of the Bayport Fire Department, and an instrumental figure in the formation of the Islip Town Volunteer Firemen's Association. Of interest was the fact that his maternal grandfather was General Regis deTrobriand, a famous Civil War hero with an illustrious military career.

In 1895, the Vanderbilts, Walter L. Suydam and family, the Rev. J.H. Prescott, and the Duke and Duchess of Marlborough were reported by the local press to be guests at the Post family estate.

Charles A. Post, the senior Post of the "Standhome" estate, strikes a distinguished yet grandfatherly pose for the camera.

Many notables of the day strolled these elegantly laid out formal gardens.

With the rhythm and expanse of the bay only a few strides away, these enclosed gardens offer ordered solitude.

"Arcadia" was the 50-acre estate of Charles F. Stoppani. Prominent was the 1888 mansion overlooking the Great South Bay, at the east foot of South Ocean Avenue. The section of the building on the right is the older, original farmhouse of William Smith, a farmer and boat builder, whose great-grandson, Hervey Garrett Smith, also loved the sea and became a strong influence in the creation of the Suffolk County Marine Museum.

Great care was taken in the plan and location of this extensive estate. The Allen Mansion on South Fairview Avenue, the present site of number 117, was described in a 1884 newspaper article as a "Queen Ann style home, with tower in front, occupying a commanding view of the South Bay beach, the ocean beyond, and that section of our beautiful village bordering on and lying to the south of the South Country Road (Middle Road)." In 1911 this home was lost to fire.

Among the familiar names of well-known owners of this beautiful home at the foot of Fairview Avenue are W.K. Post and James H. Snedecor. The home known as the "White House" also housed the local school for a two-year period when the school on Snedecor Avenue burned down in 1926.

This particular view of the "White House" emphasizes the desirable bay-view location, at the foot of Fairview Avenue in Bayport. Seen here are two young ladies, Pat Kennelly Porter on the left and Eileen Deacon Petersen on the right. Unfortunately this house was also taken by fire, in the 1940s.

The 1914 home of Walter B. Pollock at 120 Gillette Avenue was used in an advertisement aimed at continuing to draw notice from New York City vacationers, or investors. It may raise a smile now to re-read, "If you have been leading a self-centered life in a New York City flat, not knowing your next-door neighbor—if you desire, instead, healthful, enjoyable social life with your fellow beings, Bayport will be a revelation to you." And if that wasn't enough inducement, it added that, "Its moral and religious life are excellent."

One avenue to the east of Fairview is Gillette Avenue. Here on the west side of the street, at number 10, is the Gillette family home, named "the Namkee," built in 1891, for Captain Edward Gillette. Edward is the gentleman on the top step.

The "McConnell House," originally on the northwest corner of McConnell Avenue and Middle Road, was built circa 1873 as a summer home, and sold in 1906 with 50 acres for $12,000. The next phase of its life is most interesting. It was inherited by two daughters who saw fit to split it in half and move the sections to 164 and 180 McConnell wherein they would each raise their individual families. Featured in the center of this posed group are three generations of the Jurgens-Bogel family who lived there.

This interesting house at 407 Middle Road has survived as an example of adapting to each era of its history. Originally, the site was part of the Brown property acquired in 1797. The Browns eventually conveyed the properties to the Needhams, who used it as a summer boarding house in the 1880s. In the photograph shown, the house has undergone dramatic alterations under Dr. George Rice, sometime after 1912. And as a point of interest, more recently, it was the home of Hollywood's Troy Donahue, known then as Merle Johnson.

This photograph shows the Todd residence, of shipbuilding fame, on Middle Road and Marina Court. A ship's mast was used as the property's flag pole, and in the early 1900s it was used as a navigational aid to sailors on the Great South Bay. It was later moved to its prominent position in Bayport's Memorial Park. The Todds had within the walls of their house a deeper history. In 1797 William Brown purchased this land from Jeremiah Terry, and resided on this site as early as 1800. It is believed the original Brown house is incorporated within the structure we see now.

This charming house at 429 Middle Road already appears on the 1858 map of Bayport as being owned by the Lawrence Edwards family. It was bequeathed to their daughter, Elvira Weeks, along with $650 and the right to "one cow, of second choice," from the father's yard. In this circa 1885 photograph, extensive remodeling has taken place under the guidance of architect I.H. Green.

The same house, known as "Killcare Cottage," at number 429 Middle Road takes on a striking new look in this circa 1938 photograph.

Louis C. Behman purchased 30 acres on the west side of Seaman Avenue, including the existing buildings and house seen here, which was built in 1883. Today the main house is gone but some of the secondary buildings on the estate have been adaptively re-used.

As was fashionable at the time, Louis C. Behman emphasized the natural landscape with elaborate alterations to the waterways and additions of "Adirondack"-style rustic wood bridges and gazebos, creating a water park for his enjoyment.

It seems Louis C. Behman married twice, and to sisters, Marquerite (by whom he had his three children) and Evelyn. It is difficult to tell which of the two sisters this photograph shows.

Louis C. Behman, a wealthy theatrical producer from Brooklyn, transformed a Bayport land parcel into an estate he called "Lindenwaldt."

Just to the east of the old "Green" house stood this marvelous, handsomely landscaped estate built some time before 1888. "Maplewood," as it was called, was the home of Capt. Henry Richmond. The property then included a windmill and greenhouses at its site at 344 on the south side of Middle Road.

John J. Asher purchased "Maplewood" and, sometime after 1915, totally renovated the building to look like it does in this photograph. Now called "White House Farm," a conservatory was later added. This conservatory was brought out from New York City and supposedly designed by Stanford White.

In January 1889 Capt. I.S. Snedecor made provision for a new road to be cut through his farm leading to the bay. This became Snedecor Avenue, and in 1902 it continued north and now provided access from the bay all the way to Montauk Highway. This home on the southwest corner of Snedecor Avenue and Middle Road was built in 1905 by George Q. Laidlaw. With all probability, the posed family on the lawn are the Laidlaws enjoying the airy, open elegant charm of their homestead. In 1962 the United Methodist Church purchased it for use as a Sunday school. Regrettably, fire also claimed this home in 1976.

This circa 1902 I.H. Green home at 74 Snedecor Avenue was built by Fred D. Smith for Regis H. Post, who rented it out, until its sale in 1912 to John Mason of New York City. In 1946 the agriculturist, Kurt Grundwald, was living there.

Another I.H. Green home was built circa 1902 for Regis H. Post on speculation as a summer "cottage." Regis Post sold this property to nationally acclaimed actress Effie Shannon in 1912. By 1933, Miss Shannon had made 4,000 stage appearances, and John Drew and Herbert Kelsey were two of her leading men. This home boasted nine bedrooms, and it appears Herbert Kelsey also lived there a number of years.

This circa 1902 home on the west side of South Snedecor Avenue, at number 136, exemplifies the essence of comfortable elegance executed in the architectural work of I.H. Green. It was built on speculation by Regis H. Post, and in 1904 was advertised as a "cottage" on 2 acres of land, with a total of eight bedrooms, a bathroom, and two water closets, all for the summer rental price of $750. In 1922, the phone number for this address was tel. #352.

Notice the 1914 Buick in the driveway of this I.H. Green home, on the southeast corner of Middle Road and Snedecor Avenue. The home was built for I.H. Snedecor, who was one of the proprietors of what is more recently referred to as "Shand's." It was noted that on a clear day, Fire Island could be seen from the rear windows of this home.

As a wedding present for his wife, Ann Suydam, John R. Suydam purchased this home in 1854. In time he formed an even more extensive estate at the foot of Suydam Lane called "Edgewater," with this gracious home as the focal point. John Suydam was very instrumental in the creation of the St. Barnabas Church on Middle Road, just over the Sayville border. When his wife died, the name of the church, at his request, was changed to St. Ann's, as we know it today.

"Edgemere" was the name of the 29-acre Purdy estate, with property bordering on the Great South Bay and encompassing what would now be both sides of Connetquot Road. The house, which cost $9,000 to build in 1883, was situated on the south side of Middle Road exactly where Connetquot is now cut through. In the early 1920s the house was cut in half and moved to two lots on the west side of Connetquot Road, present-day houses 78 and 84.

The estate was noted for its fine flower gardens.

The carriage house was also divided and became houses 77 and 105 on the east side of Connetquot Road.

Abbie Purdy is seen here with a coachman.

This grand old house stood on the east side of Lotus Lake, and could be approached from Montauk Highway. An original section of the building existed in 1834, and there is good probability that this original structure remained while being added on to and improved when Robert Barnwell Roosevelt, an uncle of Theodore Roosevelt, purchased the 200-acre property in 1873. The house was burned in 1958.

Roosevelt included exterior design to his improvements on what we now locally refer to as the "Fortesque" estate, so named for his second wife, who lived there with her family long after his death.

Robert Barnwell Roosevelt was born in New York City in 1829, and died at his home in Bayport in 1906. Mr. Roosevelt's accomplishments in the arena of public service were numerous, and his early attention to conserving the natural environment has sparked groups today to take steps to appreciate and preserve our local resources.

Lotus Lake reflected an era of environmental awareness and appreciation.

The old mill seen here, on a circa 1913 post card, was at the south end of Lotus Lake, on what was called "Roosevelt's" pond. By 1902, and probably for some time before that, the building was used as a shop and tool shed.

Four

Leisure and Diversions:
Enjoying Who We Are

Focus on the recreational aspect of Bayport life might seem, at first glance, a bit trivial. It is, however, the very reason "city" people came our way and the reason they, in so many cases, stayed.

Two women bicyclists stand at the shoreline on Snedecor Avenue, looking west to Sayville. The attraction of the Great South Bay remains today for motorists, much as it did for bicycle riders in the year 1910.

Bicycling was probably as popular in 1904 as it is today, though helmets and spandex suits have replaced the genteel hats and long dresses of the earlier era. This circa 1904 view of South Ocean Avenue, Bayport, was taken from the front of 22 South Ocean Avenue, looking toward Middle Road. The misshapen trees are the remnants of the lopped-tree boundary markers used by early farmers to mark their property. Ocean Avenue, which prior to 1873 was called Edwards Avenue, is one of Bayport's earliest roads and was shown on the 1834 map.

Since parades were an important part of early entertainment, it seems likely that this chap, name unknown, sitting proudly astride his gaily colored, bunting-adorned bike, is heading for a Memorial Day or Fourth of July parade in Sayville. George Giroux of Bayport stands right behind the bike.

The decorated stage of Bayport High School on Snedecor Avenue is the backdrop for this "Tom Thumb Wedding" of 1932. The principals in center stage are Alma Lynch Forgione and Theodore Crampton, with members of the grammar school as attendees and wedding party members. The happy couple spent their honeymoon back in the classroom.

This very young cast of the 1903 drama, *The Irish Linen Peddlar*, stands on the stage of the Bayport Fire Hall, the building on Middle Road, just west of Snedecor and Squires store. The fire hall was used for this kind of entertainment, as well as for dances and basketball games, and generally was a center for Bayport's social life. Standing on the far left is Hervey Garrett Smith, later noted for his paintings.

The serious expression on these cardplayers lets us know that while this recreation was a diversion, it was not taken lightly. These three members of the Hahnenfeld family sit in their front yard at 89 McConnell Avenue in what is their Sunday finery.

Happy swimmers looked like this in 1910 with bathing suits that left everything to the imagination. And hats to boot!

Tennis players from early in the century relax between sets under a parasol that looks colorful. The young fellow in front seems pained over the Buster Brown suit inflicted on him in this bucolic scene in Bayport.

In the early part of this century small private bathhouses and cabanas lined the shores of the Great South Bay. These stood at the foot of Seaman Avenue. The bathers, heavily overdressed, sit and stand on one of the small docks extending into the bay.

The *Patchogue Advance* on June 14, 1901, wrote, "The people of Bayport are now looking with pride at the new dock which is in construction by the Bayport Stock Company. It will be a strong, durable structure and large enough for teams and wagons to turn around on. It will reach 200 feet into the Bay." In 1912 this dock at Gillette Avenue was completely destroyed by fire.

Boating, and particularly sailing, on the Great South Bay occupied a great deal of Bayport residents' leisure time in the warm months. This postcard of a gaff-rigged sloop, large enough to carry many people, was probably taken from either the dock at the end of Snedecor Avenue or the one at the end of Seaman Avenue. As it still is today, sailboating and sailboat races were popular and a reason for people to live in Bayport.

This painting owned by Ken and Virginia Poli of Bayport shows the artist's conception of Bill Brown's rowboat rental shack at the foot of Brown's River Road. As lonely and deserted as it appears here, it was, in fact, a lively place in the fishing season.

Winter duck hunting, a cold and lonely sport, is enjoyed by a hardy soul (unidentified) in a battery box, surrounded by decoys. His gun is at the ready, his visage is stern and vigilant, and his feet are probably freezing—all in the name of a good time.

Alone, quietly tranquil, these fellows skimming the ice get a baymen's perspective of Bayport life.

Skating here are Hazel Giroux and Evelyn Giroux Brown on Behman's Pond just off Seaman Avenue on the Behman Estate. In the background are a footbridge and an open-sided summer gazebo. This private pond was enjoyed by Bayport residents during the winter.

Fred D. Smith stands in front of his scooter *Scud* on the ice at the foot of Ocean Avenue. Seated in the cockpit is his son, Hervey Garrett Smith. Racing was an extremely cold sport but was also exhilarating from the speed reached and the proximity to the ice, which seemed to make the speeds even faster. Those who didn't race just cruised and enjoyed the quiet beauty of the frozen bay.

Isaac Howard Snedecor, who was one of the proprietors, along with his brother James, of I.S. Snedecor's Sons general store in downtown Bayport, displays his catch of ten weakfish in this circa 1910–18 photograph. The house in the background is the West house that stood at the corner of Middle Road and Bayport Avenue.

Browns River, looking north from the bay, was filled with sailboats in this 1908 photograph before motor boats became the vogue. To the left are oyster shanties and boat yards.

This very casual cabana typifies the kind of summer beach houses that dotted the shoreline of the Great South Bay in Bayport. This one stood at the foot of Ocean Avenue, but others were on Snedecor, Gerritsen, Gillette, Seaman, and Fairview Avenues and were highly prized by their owners.

This rail-less dock extended 100 feet or so into the Great South Bay, and was used not only for docking the sailboats of the era but also as a jumping off spot for swimmers such as these, shown circa 1910. Swimming, water sports, and just standing knee-deep in the bay were popular recreations. The little chap between the two women seems to be wearing a fedora.

Archie and Bud (Charles Jr.) Stien were said to own and operate this merry-go-round in Bayport and local towns around the turn of the century. Not much is known about this venture, although Shirley Schroeder and John Roberts of Blue Point, who are members of the Stien family, have heard some stories of their uncle's merry-go-round business.

The sturdy gentleman here in the foreground is George Q. Laidlaw, with friend Mr. Hicker. They are at a clam bake on August 19, 1918, at Frank Rogers Oyster Shanty, which stood at the foot of Seaman Avenue on the Great South Bay.

Five
Business and Commerce
Evolvement through the Years

The "Middle Road" bisecting the farms between Montauk Highway and the Great South Bay became, in time, the center of Bayport life. Downtown Bayport, locally called "the village," became a hub of business and social gathering.

Towering trees line Bayport village in this 1910 photograph. The view is looking east in front of the Manhattan House hotel toward Bayport Avenue. The building on the left, partly obscured by the tree, was the firehouse, which had rented store space in the front. The center building was Snedecor and Squires general store (later Shand's) and to the east of that is West's Butcher Shop. The horse-drawn buggy is tied to a hitching post on the south side of Middle Road.

A lone horse-drawn buggy stands in front of the Bayport Fire Department in this view of Middle Road, Bayport, looking west, from a postcard view circa 1910. It was taken from in front of West's Butcher Shop (not shown). The buildings, from right to left, are Snedecor and Squires General Store (later Shand's), the firehouse, and the Manhattan House. At the time this was basically the village business area.

Before motor cars clogged the streets, Bayport village on Middle Road was a quiet haven with one horse-drawn buggy and just two bicycles in front of the barber shop on the left, next to the Manhattan House. The firehouse and Snedecor and Squires General Store complete the picture, looking east toward Blue Point.

The Manhattan House hotel was built circa 1878 by John R. Terry on a piece of property sold by Warren Hawkins that was located west of Bayport Avenue on the north side of Middle Road. Terry used it as a store and residence, then sold it to Isaac S. Snedecor in 1881. By 1885 it was leased to Charles Kroll for use as a hotel and dance hall. From then until its loss to fire in August 1963 it was a hotel, bar, and restaurant. It was called Kroll's Hotel, Manhattan Hotel, National Hotel, and Manhattan House. Some of the proprietors were Julius Houser, Moses Schlesinger, Frances Haer, Henry Haer, P.J. Griffin, and Ed and Audrey Miller, to name a few.

The Roger's Ice Cream Company was located at 564 Middle Road and was started in 1904 in Bayport. Their promotional brochure said, "There is no mere luck about our success. By the skillful use of the very best materials obtainable, we produce an ice cream which meets with the full approval of the most fastidious, and by ability and willingness to fully meet all honorable competition or price we gain and retain the patronage of the most careful buyers." The ice cream was sold all along the coast, orders being sent by train.

The original Shand's Market looked like this around 1900 when it belonged to the Snedecor family. It stood on Middle Road flanked by West's Butcher Shop on the east and the firehouse on the west. The gentlemen and the dog on the porch are unidentified.

Frank Antos and William Simister are shown in the interior of the store in the early 1930s.

Arthur Shand, son of James G. and Virginia Dare Shand of Patchogue, came to Bayport in 1934 to manage the former Snedecor and Squires store, acquired by his father, who owned a general store in Patchogue. This establishment grew and prospered changing from an old-fashioned general store to a self-serve market. In 1951 Arthur Shand bought the business and it prospered under his business sense, his integrity, and his genuine interest in anyone who came through the doors. He died in 1991 at the age of ninety-one.

Arthur Shand's store, affiliated with the Royal Scarlet Stores organization, looked like this in 1935 when the Depression, in full swing, had prices at a low ebb.

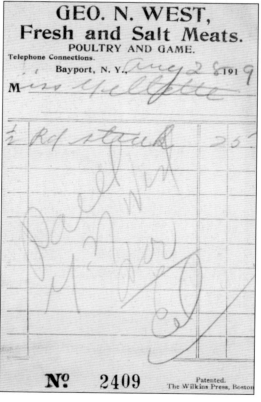

GEO. N. WEST,
Fresh and Salt Meats.
POULTRY AND GAME.
Telephone Connections.
Bayport, N. Y., *Aug 28 1919*

M*iss Mellette*

½ Rd steak   25

Nº 2409   Patented.
The Wilkins Press, Boston

George N. West, a resident of Setauket, opened his 22-by-25-foot butcher shop in June of 1889 on land he leased from Isaac Snedecor, just east of Snedecor's general store (which in 1934 became Shand's Market). The building stayed there until sometime after 1946 when it was moved to 129 Kensington Avenue to become a residence. An article written about this butcher business in 1914 indicated it was a thriving endeavor with six people working for West. The billhead shown has half a pound of round steak for 25¢ and indicates "telephone connections," which meant telling the operator, "Give me West's butcher store."

Mrs. Edmond Wicks had the building on the left converted to use as an oyster house early in the 1880s. Subsequently it was used by the Wicks brothers as a candy store and an ice cream parlor. From 1889 to 1892 this building served as Bayport's third post office, with Charles W. Tuttle serving as postmaster. In 1893 it became the residence of I. Scudder Snedecor.

William Mantha Company and Garage sat on the corner of Middle Road and Bayport Avenue and combined a machine shop with a budding car repair business. By 1910, 460,000 cars were on the road and were revolutionizing transportation. The William Mantha Company was one of the many garages opened on Long Island for the maintenance of the new cars. Besides providing Monogram Oil and greases, Michelin tires, and Mobil oil gasoline, Mantha's was an official agent for Reo automobiles.

A postcard view of Bayport's village on the Middle Road, circa 1935, shows a Ralston grocery store, managed by Sam Monsell of Blue Point. Three of the cars are identified as a 1932 Ford Roadster (left), a 1933 Ford (right), and a 1933 Chevrolet (in the background). The view looks west toward Sayville.

At the eastern extent of the downtown hub, the Moon Rise restaurant, locally known as Ma Moon's, was run by Minne Moon, wife of George Moon. German-style cooking was served and much beer was poured. Locals came there to play cards in the evening and to socialize. Dinners were 50¢ and up. Prior to being a restaurant there was a blacksmith shop on the site. Local historian Eva Gillette wrote in 1949, "The blacksmith shop in this town stood where the building now stands and this shop was owned by George E. Smith." Smith opened a shop on the site on August 8, 1886. It was listed in a business directory in 1911–12 and on a map in 1915. In 1938 it was shown to be a restaurant.

The respective homes of "Doc" Neveloff's pharmacy and Bill Stuart's plumbing shop were photographed in 1938 on the Middle Road in Bayport village.

Aaron "Doc" Neveloff ran the only drug store in Bayport for years, dispensing wisdom and prescriptions and, according to those who knew him well, performing quiet good deeds in the community. The drug store, located at 584 Middle Road, also had a soda fountain—a rarity now, but commonplace in the 1930s and '40s.

Bill Stuart started his plumbing business in a small shop in the front of the old firehouse and later moved to 582 Middle Road in the heart of Bayport's village, now the site of Spotlite Beauty Salon. Old timers remember that plumbing fixture in the window and the general disarray of the shop!

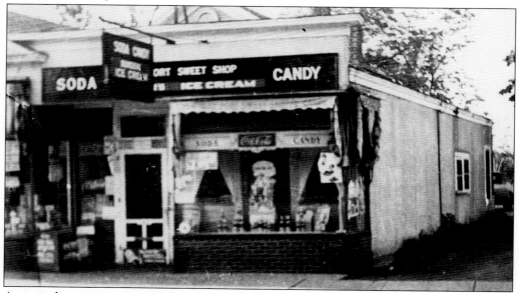

Among the many proprietors of this candy store/luncheonette, Emile Stoll was the first, followed by Bill Jewett and Howard Shene. It was the hub of gossip some say, and the morning meeting place for both local working men and those grabbing a cup of coffee and a morning paper, which Howard "reserved" for regular customers. "Mac," the local street-sweeper and the Manhattan House's sole tenant, could be easily tempted into restepping his former vaudevillian routines with just a throw of salt upon the store floor. Residents today still fondly remember 5¢ cokes, egg creams, and hand-packed ice cream.

This shop at 566 Middle Road, now the office of Attorney Warren Siska, was the barber shop of Jacob Iverson in 1938. Subsequently it served as a real estate office and as an accountant's place of business.

Further west at 396 Middle Road, nestled among residences, stood the Bayport Hotel, with Henry L. Stokes as proprietor. Mr. and Mrs. Francois Geille became the owners circa 1916 and ran the hotel/restaurant under the name "L'Azur" for the next eighteen years. In 1938 Gustav and Maria Blocker bought the hotel and in 1949 added a restaurant known as the Colonial Inn. The Blockers converted the inn into a convalescent home in 1953 and changed the name to Pleasant Gardens. It is currently run by their son, Julius Blocker.

Nowhere in Bayport are you far from the Great South Bay. Business also focused there; Myer's Railways was on Brown's River between Bayport and Sayville.

Frank Rogers (the gentleman shown at the extreme right) had an oyster shanty on the Bayport side of Brown's River circa 1900. Brown's River is the divider between the towns of Bayport and Sayville. The watch boat *Green*, with Washington Green as captain, patrolled the oyster beds to monitor the activities of oyster "poachers." Directly behind the horse and wagon, the main land transportation, is a huge pile of oyster shells often sold or given away to pave roads and driveways in the local area.

Workers handle oysters at the Brown Brothers Oyster Business, circa 1902, on Brown's River. Edmund and Charles Brown bought 2.5 acres of property from Warren Hawkins in 1890 and in 1891 bought an adjacent 20 acres from John and Harriet Suydam to establish the business. In 1911 Brown Brothers sold out to Seal Ship & Oyster System, who then sold out in 1915 to the Blue Point Company, probably the most successful oyster business in the area.

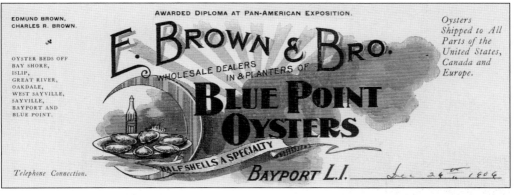

Back to the "village" and up to 147 Bayport Avenue, a business for the major part of forty years was the Hawkins Bottling Company. Starting in 1880 as a partnership of George Bishop and Frank Johnson, their trade was in gingerine, somewhat similar to gingerale. Later they added sarsaparilla, lemon, and plain soda to their stock. The bottles used are collector's items today. At the time they were all returnable with the company's message explicitly stating "You are buying the contents, not the container." Shown in this 1905 picture are Clifton Hawkins on the wagon and Charlie Smith seated on the horse.

Further north on Bayport Avenue, just south of the railroad tracks, stands an inviting restaurant, shown here as it looked with its outbuildings still on the property. The barn has been moved to the Islip Grange restoration site. Formerly, built as an inn in 1880 by Charles and William Frieman (Charles later owned the Shoreham Hotel on the bay in Sayville), it was called Frieman's Hotel.

W.J. Shady leased the Frieman Hotel in 1910, changed the name to the Fiat Inn, and ran it until 1920 when it was sold by Mary Frieman to Gene Amann, who called it Amann's Bayport House and stayed in business until 1953. It was then sold to Hans Rohde, who entitled it Hans and Katy's (his sister). In 1969, Katy's niece, Ursula Weiss, inherited the property and operated it until 1980, when Diana and Willie Calderale bought the property and started the successful "Bayport House Ristorante." This photograph depicts a 1910 view.

This wonderful horse and buggy belonged to Gene Amann when he was the owner of Gene Amann's Restaurant and Hotel (see above). It was used to transport passengers on the Long Island Railroad from the station to his watering hole. The carriage lantern is a beauty.

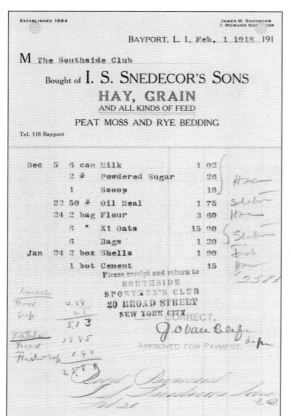

This billhead from I.S. Snedecor's Sons, dated February 1, 1918, is directed to "The Southside Club" in Oakdale, a sportsman's club reserved for well-to-do hunters and fishermen.

In 1904, Snedecor and Squires bought a plot of ground on the north side of the Long Island Railroad tracks and east of Bayport Avenue and had a large warehouse built to house Snedecor and Squires Grain and Feed Store. This business was run as an extension of their general store on Middle Road. Deliveries were made to the warehouse from a special side track of the railroad and then delivered locally by horse and wagon or by truck.

Along those same railroad tracks, between Snedecor and Oakwood Avenues, Clarence E. Hibbard and John Sawyer Jr. established the Bayport Barrel Company in 1904. The company made a specialty of barrels for the oyster trade, particularly for the world-famous Blue Point oyster business. The building covered almost half an acre on the north side of the tracks, and by 1914, under Hibbard, with Frank Corey as foreman, fifteen men were employed turning out 100,000 barrels a season. By 1938 this facility was gone and the site was occupied by the Gulf Oil Company.

The flower business has been a major factor in Bayport's economy. In May of 1906, Julius Chevally purchased this greenhouse property and residence, on the south side of Montauk Highway and east of Gillette Avenue, from George M. Biggs, who had established one of the earliest commercial greenhouse businesses in the area in 1899. Biggs had leased it to Chevally in 1904 for five years with an option to buy at any time. By 1938 there were eight large greenhouses and a second, more elegant home on the property. Today, the Bayport Adult Home occupies this second house and condominiums are being built on the former greenhouse area, which wrapped around the homestead.

Shown here are Norma, Paul, Gisbert, and Maria Auwaeter. The Bayport Flower Houses, one of Bayport's most successful growers, have been in business since 1932 under the care of the Auwaeter family—first by Maria and Paul Auwaeter, then by Gisbert, their son, and now by a combination of Gisbert and his son Karl.

This 1945 aerial view of the Bayport Flower Houses shows the "big house" and the proximity to the railroad, which made it easy to bring in soft coal for heating the greenhouses and for shipping the boxes of cut flowers to New York City. The early emphasis on the wholesale selling of flowers has declined and now the retail shop on the premises is the mainstay.

In a time around 1936, when no one pumped his own gasoline, Herb Lipson stands ready to serve at his Mobil gas pumps in front of Lipson's Service Station on Montauk Highway. Most wonderful is the price of gasoline—15¢ a gallon.

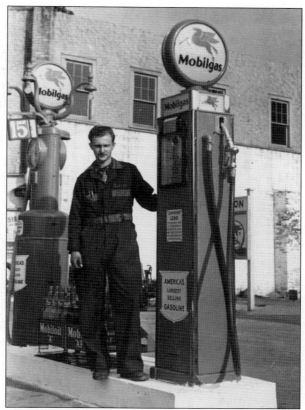

To the west of Lipson's Service Station stood this refreshment stand, a precursor of today's convenience stores which are so ubiquitous. Standing in front are Marjorie Brown on the left and Mildred Hollins Stevens on the right.

Today's Bayport Aerodrome Field was started just after World War II and was called Davis Field after its founder, James Davis, a Blue Point house mover, and his son Curtis, an avid aviation enthusiast. In 1953 George Edwards bought the field and it became Edwards Airport.

In May of 1978 the *Suffolk County News*, a local paper, announced that under Supervisor Peter F. Cohalan, Islip Town with a federal grant of $776,250 bought the field and renamed it the Bayport Aerodrome, a living museum where exhibits could be rolled out and flown. The only other museum of this type is in Bedfordshire, England, for the Shuttlesworth collection.

Six
Institutions and Organizations:
The Soul of a Hamlet

Paramount in the history of any small town are the institutions and organizations that are the cohesive factors in the stability, the growth, and the social life of the community.

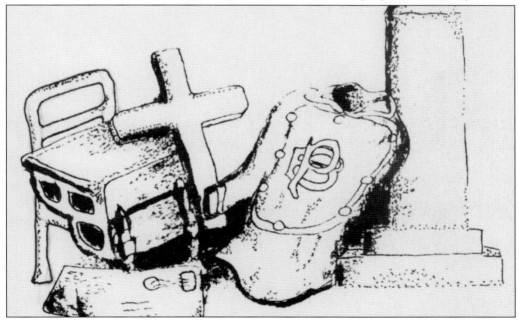

Bayport's social and service institutions are viewed within the following pages, in order of their creation or original building: Bayport Schools, 1819; the Bayport Post Office, 1870; the Bayport Methodist Church, 1872; the Bayport Fire Department, 1891; Bayport Memorial Park, 1945; Camp Edey, 1948; and the Bayport Heritage Association, 1983.

The first schoolhouse in Bayport was built in 1819 and burned down circa 1825. This line drawing, sketched by Mary Jones Gillette, interprets what the second "one-room" schoolhouse might have looked like in 1825.

This second building served the community from then until 1867, when it was moved to a new site on the northeast corner of Bayport Avenue and Middle Road. In 1907, William L. Mantha obtained the property for use as a machine and automobile repair shop, as shown in the photograph. The small complex of buildings which eventually included a show room was lost to fire on Tuesday, April 4, 1967.

The entire graduation class of the Bayport High School in 1889 sits for this photograph in formal dress. They are, from left to right, Clifton Hawkins, Edna Rhodes, Warren Dodge, Yetta Overton, Gil Gillette, and William Smith. At the time, the principal was Millard H. Packer and his assistant was Emily Benjamin. Both of them also served as teachers along with Inez Overton.

CLOSING EXERCISES.
CLASS OF '89.
INTERMEDIATE DEPARTMENT,
OF THE
BAYPORT PUBLIC SCHOOL,
IN THE
→✠M. ✢ E. ✢ CHURCH,✠←
BAYPORT, LONG ISLAND.
THURSDAY EVENING, JUNE 20, 1889.

In the early 1890s, as the Bayport community continued to grow, it became evident that a larger schoolhouse was needed. Plans began for a new building on a new site on November 20, 1894, and on January 12, 1895, the school trustees, George L. Myers, Charles G. Bishop, and George W. Gilbert, purchased a 2-acre tract on Snedecor Avenue from Mary E. Gillette. The new building was dedicated on March 18, 1895. The building had five rooms to accommodate two hundred students and cost $6,206.05 to build. In 1895 there were 134 pupils enrolled and the school budget was $3,681.00. On the night of February 5, 1926, the building was destroyed by fire.

This photograph, taken before 1926 when the wooden schoolhouse burned, shows the abundance of trees and paucity of houses on Snedecor Avenue, south of the building. The two young girls on the seesaw are Mae Huston on the left and Lillian Stuart (later Chevally) on the right. Lillian was the daughter of Bill Stuart, a local plumber and story-teller.

The teacher of this 1911 third and fourth grade Bayport elementary class is Florence Parker, who later married James Snedecor, a longtime and prominent Bayport resident. In this photograph are Ed Frieman, Rudy Veverka, Nat Norton, Marion Stoll, Winnie Dedrick, Carleton L'Hommedieu, Charles Brown, John Hodge, Mary Sullivan, and Al Wageli—all names wonderfully familiar to vintage Bayporters.

Among those posed on the front steps of Bayport's school, circa 1915, are Jennie Houdek, Winnie Dedrick, Carleton L'Hommedieu, Gladys Giroux, Edward Frieman, Mable Adler, Mildred Stoll, Nat Norton, Louella Drake, and Marion Stoll, and Robert Frost.

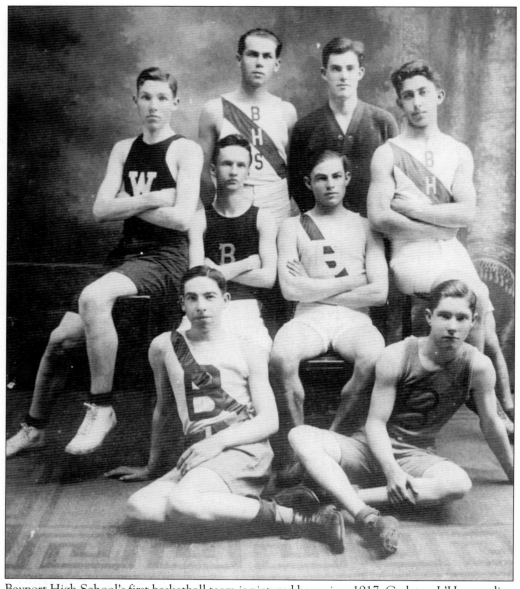

Bayport High School's first basketball team is pictured here circa 1917. Carleton L'Hommedieu is seated on the left in front and directly behind him is Ed Frieman; the others are unidentified.

Bayport High School's girls' basketball team of 1921–22 poses for a team photo. This, apparently, is the entire squad outfitted in their uniforms. In the front row, from left to right, are Eleanor Smith, Margaret Bogel, and Regina Sherwood. The second row has Gertrude Gerety, Barbara Pavlik, and Audrey Platt. The coach is Johnny Burns.

In 1932 the Bayport High School girls' basketball team was coached by a Mr. Alsdorf, shown here on the left in the back row. The principal at the time was Stanley Platt, who is standing to the far right. Marion Snedecor, who later married Cy Beebe of Sayville, sits in the front row second from the left. The photograph came from the 1932 *Bayport Scholar*, volume 1, number 5, which was then the school paper.

The Bayport School building dedicated on November 3, 1927, was both an elementary school and a four-year high school. The first graduates in June of 1928 were Edmond Brown, Hazel Fairchild, Helen Smith, Mary Norton, and Francis Kelly. On August 5, 1930, the $50,560 budget was passed unanimously by twenty-six voters.

This is the site of the first post office in 1870. The building had been moved from Blue Point by William B. Arthur, who owned and operated a general store in his home. Mr. Arthur was postmaster from 1870 to 1885. The building still stands today, as then, north of the railroad tracks on the east side of Bayport Avenue. It is in close proximity to our current post office, which is located on Montauk Highway just east of Bayport Avenue.

Pictured here is the home of the Bayport Post Office from 1895 to 1914. Edward J. Woods was postmaster at the time. The Woods brothers also operated a real estate office here. The original building was located on the south side of Middle Road at the present location of Morgan Lane. John A. Hicks purchased this property in 1851 and sold it to John Morgan of New York City in 1887. The building was later moved south to 2 Morgan Lane on the west side.

Through the years the post office was housed in various other locations on Middle Road. This location within the right section of the Howell Building served the community in 1948 until 1955. City mail delivery service was started in 1956 during the tenure of George Dedrick. Since 1980, the post office has been located on Montauk Highway.

The highlight of Memorial Day, 1976, in Bayport was the unveiling of a monument in front of the Bayport Post Office. The inscription written by Peter Desmond said: "The old village church. Silent at rest, the calm bay waters, lapping the shore. This is my hometown. This is my country—free forever free." From left to right are Assemblyman Paul Harenberg, Supervisor Peter Cohalan, Peter Desmond, the Rev. Derrick Moon, and postmaster Stanley Orenkewicz.

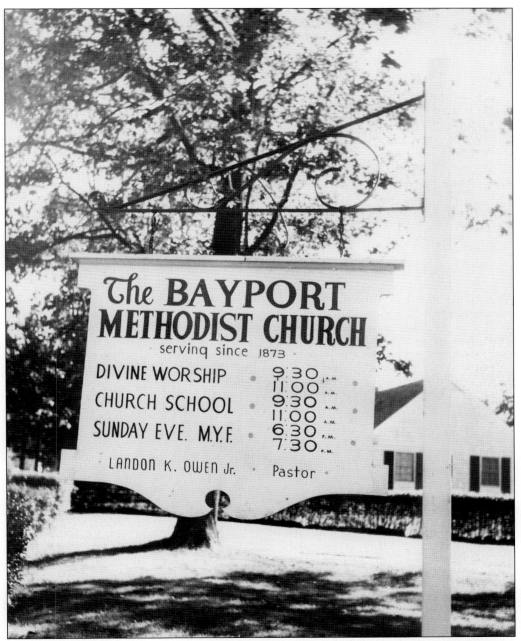

The sign board in front of the Bayport Methodist Church, circa 1961, showed Landon K. Owen as the minister. He was young, energetic, and charismatic, and church attendance soared. The Bayport United Methodist Church is, and always has been, the only church in Bayport, and today maintains a congregation of over five hundred.

An attractive post card view shows the Bayport Methodist Episcopal Church, now known as the Bayport United Methodist Church, built in 1873. The entire cost of the 32-by-50-foot building was $3,500. Reverend S. Kristeller was the first of the forty-six ministers who have served this country church, which captures the small community charm of Bayport.

The parsonage, adjacent to the church, was built in 1896 and is still in use at this time by Pastor Noel Koestline and her husband. It has four bedrooms, a dining room, a living room, a large kitchen, and a great front porch.

Individuals in the Methodist Church boys' choir, circa 1903, proved impossible to identify, but the two women pictured are Mrs. Parks, the minister's wife, and Edna Jackson, organist.

Shown here is an interior view of the Bayport Methodist Church, circa 1938–40. This was the time when the Reverend Arthur Tedcastle was the popular minister of the church. He was succeeded around 1940 by Alson J. Smith. The organ with the pipes is long gone and the original pew seats were replaced in 1995.

In 1927, the church, as shown above, added an extension consisting of a Sunday school room, a kitchen, and an office; stained glass windows were soon to be installed.

This interior view of the Bayport Methodist Church shows the new pews installed in 1995, each one carrying a small plaque from the family that financed the pew. The hanging tapestries on the front and back walls were designed by Margaret Erath and are changed to reflect the church calendar.

The Bayport Methodist Church looks like this today in this photograph of the west side. The parish hall on the right is used for church suppers, some Sunday school services, as a polling place, and as an auditorium for a play school in the church. The sign in front points to a thrift shop tucked in the back. The church spire holds a bell used on Sunday mornings and a carillon dedicated to the memory of Lucille and Arthur Shand. It plays twice a day. In 1998 there will be a year-long celebration of the 125 years of the church's existence.

The original Bayport Firehouse was built in 1892 in the village on the north side of Middle Road, west of, and now part of, the Bayport Village Market, formerly Shand's Market. One of the features of the building was that on the west front there was a retail store, whose rent was to defray part of the costs of the newly formed fire department. Sometime in the early 1920s the store was eliminated to make room for additional fire equipment. The fire department moved to its new and present headquarters on Railroad Avenue in 1956.

This two-wheeled horse-drawn hose cart was the first piece of apparatus purchased by the fire department in 1891, and predates the firehouse. It carried 500 feet of hose. As an incentive, the first farmer and horse to arrive in response to a fire call received $1 for pulling the cart. In October 1991, the department located and restored a cart identical to this original. The cart is usually on display at special fire department events.

The first hook and ladder truck was bought in the spring of 1896 for $75 and sold in 1906 to the St. James Fire Department. For thirty-five years Bayport's department financially supported itself through fund-raisers and the generous donations of Bayport residents. By 1926 the village had grown and the demand for better and more modern equipment became urgent. A Fire District was formed so that apparatus and equipment could be purchased by taxing real estate property.

This early parade photograph, taken in 1897, shows the original department uniform. The red shirt, white pants, and blue hat are as proudly worn today as they were then. Bayport is one of the only departments in the country to have retained their original volunteer fireman's uniform design.

Sometime in the early 1920s, the storefront featured in the front of the firehouse building was eliminated to make room for additional fire equipment. In 1956 the fire department moved to its new and present headquarters on Railroad and Snedecor Avenues.

This circa 1914 photograph shows one of Bayport Fire Department's earliest racing teams still using a hose cart. West's Butcher Shop and Snedecor's Grocery Store, later Shand's, can be seen next to department headquarters in the village.

Bayport was the Suffolk County Tournament Champions in 1914 at Riverhead. The department chief was James H. Snedecor, the track captain was W. Kintzing Post, and the nozzle man was Emile Stoll.

The Bayport Fire Department hosted this tournament on August 31, 1932. It was held on Connetquot Road. Some noteworthy facts were recorded that day. Impressively, 1,770 Fire Department Association members paraded, representing 43 fire departments with 144 pieces of apparatus. An early morning heavy storm began the day, but the skies then cleared, and the day ended with a full eclipse of the sun in the afternoon.

The firehouse was renovated in the early 1920s and later housed the motorized apparatus as two truck bays were added.

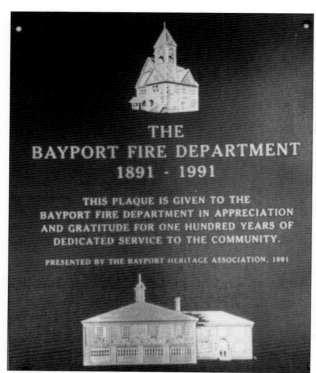

On the occasion of the 100th birthday of the Bayport Fire Department, the Bayport Heritage Association presented this plaque to the organization and it is now displayed in the second-floor meeting room.

On August 15, 1891, a number of Bayport residents met in the old schoolhouse to organize a fire department, and Charles A. Post became their first chief. One hundred years later, this photograph was taken in celebration of the department's 100th anniversary in 1991—"100 years of dedicated service."

Before there was a Memorial Park in Bayport, Decoration Day Services were held in front of the firehouse, which was on Middle Road next to Shand's store. The firemen, in their unique fire uniforms, stand at attention while the crowd mills and the oratory flows. Behind the speakers is a plaque dedicated to the veterans of World War I; the plaque disappeared when the firehouse became part of Shand's.

The first Veteran's Memorial board in Bayport stood on Middle Road in front of George West's house, to the east of his butcher shop. It displayed the names of those who served during World War I, and remained there until after World War II, when the Bayport Memorial Park was established.

Just after World War II the Bayport Memorial Park was established on the corner of the Esplanade and Middle Road. This donated boulder was located by Charlie Dedrick in a sand and gravel operation owned by Sam Barnett in the Setauket area and was moved for $100 by Davis Brothers of Blue Point. The plaque was attached and plans were formulated for landscaping and beautifying the area.

This huge flag, donated to the Memorial Park by the Eastern Federal Bank of Blue Point and its manager, Nellie Watterson, was raised for Memorial Day of 1988 and disappeared that night forever. Holding the flag are, from left to right, Connie Haab, Grace and Carl Stoye, Nellie Watterson, Charlie Bogel (founder of the Memorial Park), Stanley Orenkewicz, Alden and Flo Olsson, and the late Marge Bogel. Stanley Orenkewicz has long served as president of the Memorial Park Association. As master of ceremonies at Memorial Services, he has conveyed warm sensitivity and community awareness.

The centerpiece of the Bayport Memorial Park is this black granite memorial that has four plaques commemorating those from Bayport who served their country in wars from the Revolutionary War through Vietnam. Two benches, shrubbery, and seasonal plantings highlight the appearance of the area—a favorite spot for visitors to stop and rest and reflect.

This obelisk was placed in the Bayport Memorial Park in 1986 as a celebration of the 200th year of Bayport's existence. Money was raised from every organization in town and from private individuals. The monument is inscribed on all four sides with pictorial designs created by Denise McFadden and Mary Jones Gillette and with the well-chosen words of Don Weinhardt. The flag pole to the rear is almost 90 feet tall and was once the mast of an ocean-going racing yacht.

Camp Edey occupies wooded land bordering the chain-like system of ponds, called the Sans Souci Lakes, which empty south into Browns River, and ultimately into the Great South Bay. These ponds were altered into their present shape by early settlers who worked off the ponds, using them as cranberry bogs in the summer, and cutting ice blocks from them in the winter. The property became part of the Greene Estate, and it was from this estate that the combined districts of Long Island Girl Scouts purchased the property in 1948, calling it Camp Edey.

Camp Edey began providing girls a summer camp experience, in a preserved and private environment, consisting of 102 acres of wetlands. Girls from other locations enjoyed a taste of Bayport's environment, as did many of our own Bayport girls. They share fond memories of youthful joy.

The Memorial Day parade in Bayport starts on Connetquot Road and winds up in the Bayport Memorial Park. Bayport Heritage Association members proudly display their banner and vintage costumes. Carol Fuchsius is holding the banner on the left, and Don Weinhardt is on the right.

This 1983 photograph shows the Bayport Heritage Association's first directors and officers. From left to right are as follows: (seated) Edith Miller, Marion Beebe, Flo Olsson, June Gillette, Irma Reilly, and Carole Pichney; (standing) Mel Leach, Alden Olsson, Stanley Orenkewicz, and Don Weinhardt.

In 1984 Meadow Croft, the Roosevelt estate, was in this badly run-down state and restoration seemed a far-off dream.

By 1996 the Meadow Croft exterior was almost completed and with a coat of yellow paint resembled the 1910 estate—the goal of the restoration.

This view of the heirloom garden at Meadow Croft, with the carriage house under restoration in the background, is as seen in 1994. A Colonial Revival garden, restored by Heritage volunteers, serves not only to beautify, but also to educate. Denise McFadden, in costume, leads the tour for the Sayville Garden Club.

These Heritage members are, from left to right, Chip Rudiger, Marilyn Goldsmith, Ann Marie Roberts, Flo Olsson, Denise McFadden, and Don Weinhardt. They are dressed in summer attire costume, which adds to the flavor of special events.

The Bayport Heritage Association was formed in 1983 and today is a burgeoning organization with over 450 members dedicated to the preservation of the history of Bayport, with an extensive collection of archival photographs, vintage clothing, artifacts, and books. Through the years since 1983 the association has been particularly active in the restoration of Meadow Croft, a John Ellis Roosevelt summer home on the border of Bayport and Sayville, and has received credit for the initiative to save the estate to become an historical museum. On this site members have restored and maintain a prize-winning heirloom garden under the painstaking guidance of garden designer Dan Pichney. The organization provides lectures and resources—educational, historical, environmental, and social programs and services for the community and interested public. Two annual events that have become community traditions are the BHA spring yard sale and the autumn house tour. The organization's previous publication, *Bayport—Fading Views* (1986), has also drawn favorable community response. Don and Carol Weinhardt, residents of Bayport since 1979 with a strong interest in local history, started the organization in 1983 and have both served as presidents once or twice and on the Board of Directors, always moving the organization toward its current strength as a preserver of local history.